MOOG

Moonbathing

VALERIE LAWS

PETERLOO POETS

First published in 2003
by Peterloo Poets
The Old Chapel, Sand Lane, Calstock, Cornwall PL18 9QX, U.K.

A catalogue record for this book is available
from the British Library

ISBN 1-904324-02-9

Printed and bound by Antony Rowe Ltd, Eastbourne

ACKNOWLEDGEMENTS

Are due to the editors of the following journals: *Iron Magazine, Haiku Quarterly, Writing Women, Fatchance, Outposts, Other Poetry, Odyssey;* and anthologies, *Under the Bridge* (ed Penny Smith), *Star Trek – the Poems* (ed. Valerie Laws), *An Enduring Flame* (ed. Wendy Bardsley), *Golden Girl* (ed. Alan C. Brown); and the author of the book *100 Days on Holy Island* (Peter Mortimer, Mainstream Press, 2002). Seven of the poems were published in *For Crying Out Loud,* her joint collection with Kitty Fitzgerald (Iron Press 1994). 'Don't put your daughter into space, Mrs Kirk' was a prizewinner in the National Poetry Competition, 'The Woman whose Husband mistook her for a hat' in an *Envoi* competition. 'The Heart does not break...' toured London, Tokyo, and New York as part of the *One Heart, One World* International Exhibition.

Thanks and love to Peter Mortimer; also to Jenny Lewis, U.A. Fanthorpe and Rosie Bailey for their support, and to the Tutors of the Creative Writing MA, University of Northumbria at Newcastle.

For my children, Robin & Lydia,
and my parents, Sheila and Lindsay
with love

Contents

Nantucket, 1810

Laudanum strokes me throat to womb, warm
as a lover, my lover, who's cold as the sea
and wet, wild wind. Somewhere, nowhere,
his harpoon thrusts into the hot muscle
of the whale's heart, the final spurt
of scalding blood and sperm oil splattering
the white foam, his head. All I have of him
is the memory of his face before the sea
scoured it, three children born three years
apart, and six inches of cold hard plaster.

'He's-at-homes', we call them, we whalers' wives,
perhaps already widows months ago; we work
as both man and wife, mother and father, visit
each other, talk business, wear our Quaker black,
make money. At night, like them, I close my lips
around the bottle's neck, feel that rush of heat,
and reach for him, my he's-at-home, hard
but dead, the only part death cannot stiffen
when a body rolls with the humpback waves.

Deeper than laudanum, deeper than harpoons
can penetrate, deeper than six inches can reach
in me, thick water closes over him in my dreams.
He may come back, briefly, a stranger, older,
rougher, the real man with his hot demands
seeming less real than the figure of his manhood
which shares my nights, my bed, my life,
which never leaves me for that whore, the sea.

'I didn't want to do it'

(inscribed by a Roman soldier on Hadrian's Wall)

The weight of not wanting lies on this land
like pabulum on a sea-sick stomach. Here
where the whin sill heaved itself stiffly up,
groaning, from its bed, the wall was whacked down
like a rod on the back of Northumberland;
and now, as larks hoist themselves into the sky,
summer makes a grudging appearance, and even sheep
persistently run away from the farmers, it endures,
a monument to Roman lack of enthusiasm.

After all, for every zealot, conqueror, leader,
there are thousands who would really rather not.
In the trenches of the Great War almost every man
would have preferred to be somewhere else,
while the reluctance of the Imperial Chinese
can be seen from the moon.

All over the world, and maybe on other worlds,
people are doing things they don't want to do.
perhaps the mass of their unwillingness is the
dark matter slowing the expansion of the universe;

perhaps pi, scratched into the fabric of the cosmos,
is God's infinite grumble.

Gaudi

Not a straight line in sight, or in his head;
instead, the great slotted cones of the towers
of Sagrada Familia, grating the golden light
like cheese –
the parabola of stoneflight, the swooping
hyperbola of roof-saddle –
the way sandstone melts under the wash
of waves, as bones erode and crumble like shells –
the way bones in a limb meet, chaperoned by sinew,
cushioned by fluid, just kissing
as through a veil;
the agony of the tree
forced into squared lines, Christ
nailed into a semblance of right angles –
the way pillars soar and divide like beeches,
beeches wear like grey sandstone,
sandstone articulates like bone, bone
sprouts into pillars of slender grace.

Surefooted he moved through his own
thoughts, growing them around him, his
shabby clothes stony with dust, until thirst
for the Mass drove him out, to blunder
into the truly surreal;
the straight lines, the steel tracks,
the steel tram; the crushing of bone,
the parabola of blood from torn arteries,
the nave of ribs pierced with light; nailed
to a rectangular bed in a pauper's ward,
unrecognized, dying
while the builders scrambled through the cells
of his mind, searching for him.

Christmas Island

He had no smell
although he never washed
(occasionally put Omo in the bath,
and got in, with his socks on)
and sweated in the hot sun, scrambling
over the cliffs, his dangerous old shotgun
pointing over his shoulder.
Thin, almost toothless, brown, with grizzly beard
and ape's bright, pushed-in eyes,
his bedroom carpeted with dust and filthy dishes
and suitcases of antique pornography,
(he added instruments of torture with a biro)
kept fit on fags, sugar and strong coffee,
he had no smell at all; we put it down
to Christmas Island, where he was irradiated
in the atom tests. Others got cancers, he
was preserved, like a supermarket strawberry
with a long shelf-life and no taste.

He told us, "The Americans got goggles. We
were told, cover your eyes. I could see
all the bones in my hand when it went off."

But he had no chance of Government compensation
for loss of body odour and a hand x-ray
branded onto his retina.

Standing on Swastikas

In the bath house where they thought to wash away
the dust, becoming dust themselves,
we stand on swastikas, symbols of eternity,
warmed now by sun as then by furnaces.
They must have thought that world would last forever;
only buildings stand, preserved for us to look at. Those shapes
that jolt the eye, black spiders, full of movement,
writhe on the pavement, uncrushable
however many tread on them. But the people, about to be
engulfed by choking fumes, blistering heat, and
darkness, stood here, bare feet on hot tiles,
as we stand now, where houses grow from
the rock like coral, amber, pink, butterscotch, white,
and swimming pools glitter like turquoise tesserae:
below a sun caught in a net of lemons, the scent
of jasmine, orange and wisteria; stood here,
in Herculanium, as the first flakes of ash
fell gentle as wisteria blossom, easily brushed away
from those whirling crosses, spiky and alive.

A Marriage of Minds

(after Shakespeare's sonnet 116)

Let me not to the marriage of true minds
admit impediment. If love's not love
that alters when it alteration finds,
then I did not love you. I must have lied
for all those years we shared our lives, a bed;
I should be happy now to step aside
so you can say to her what once you said
to me. For I have found you altered,
become a person that I never knew.
Hit by your treachery, my love has faltered,
and so is proved, no less than yours, untrue.
You said I was your soul-mate. Now it's she,
unless you have twin souls to match two faces,
or a new soul that in mid-life replaces
the old love with a younger blonde. For me,
if I can't love, I must try not to hate
either you or her. True minds can't mate
in a bed of lies, as you will learn too late.

GSOHnnet

'Attractive guy, GSOH, and OHAC, seeks
female, no ties.' You see the ad, and fix
a date by phone, hoping for laughs, some sex.
Just when you think it's going to be excellent,
you look down at the mustard towelling socks
he's going to take off last. You can't relax.
You know, he takes them off, and something stinks
like camembert gone off, and you make tracks.
You need much more than nights in, out, and jokes,
but if you believe the ads, there must be stacks
of men and women enjoying country walks
while in a state of permanent hysterics.
The world must be a truly happy place,
where every lonely heart has a smiling face.

'Life's too short to stuff a mushroom'

Fête de champignons farcies –
here, they know it takes many lives
to celebrate and explore the filling
of those plump spaces,
smelling of truffle, soil and mist.

In ecstatic festival, this town
takes to woods and fields,
suntanned fingers softened by dew
seeking and stroking skin
smooth as a baby's arm.

The royal wings of the skate-like parasol,
the curve of the chanterelle, the cep,
the slippery oyster, fat puffball
with its tight mouth dribbling
a thread of smoky spores.

The removal of the stipe, tubby
as an elephant's leg, or slender
as a supermodel's thigh; the pale navel,
the breaking of brittle flesh
moist and frangible. Then the invasion
of the fungus, the stuffing, the covering
of the pink gills, bleeding brown rust.

Gently, packing each crevice with care,
or slapdash in great dollops; hard
little nuggets or lush trowellings
of – what? Pungent green herbs,
white cheeses oozing milk, blue-veined
as a nursing breast; garlic pearly and hot,
tomatoes bursting with juice and seeds,
giving their all, splitting their skins.

Praise the Lord and Pass the Ammunition

The rainbow arch hangs in space
at Lindisfarne, a cannonball's leap
frozen in stone. Hail and rain rattle
the walls like shot, the sea keeps up
its cavalry charge. Cows graze
salt-bleached grass, descendants
of those spared by the monks
who spent more on gunpowder
than parchment.

Cold as steel, the salty air
that cramped their fingers
as they hefted the sacks
of *black meal, protection
against the devil's reivers.

Within, by the fire, Eadfrith
lit the pages of the gospels,
on calf-skin pricked with needles,
tattooed with inks. So slow a fuse
burning in red and gold, his truth
needing a little help from the gunsmith,
shielding the spark, so easily flaring up
and catching hold.

*Black meal; flour paid as protection money on the
Northumbrian/Scots border: giving term blackmail.

Carving an icy horse.

A spiked wheel like a spur pecks the frozen surface of the
thick block, tracing the sweep of mane, the prick of ears, the
moon-curve of cheek. The drawing lifts to show its negative
etched, deepened by the chisel, which ploughs the paths
again. Snow, salt-white, churns up in a wet furrow as it goes.
Then the chainsaw, its teeth chattering, cuts each straight
section of each curve right through. Sliced chunks fall away
and shatter. The icy horse is an equine prism now, until a
tiny spade digs out the detail, flying strands of hair, slick with
snow-laden wind, the white eye with its cut-glass corners.
The horse stands up, a huge glossy chess piece, its face all
planes like a Greek war horse in armour. Now the chisel
carves facets like those on chandelier crystals, finer and
finer, flat planes becoming round, until the ears are cones,
the face a slender vase, the nostrils commas snorting cold
steam. The hose washes the slush away and the horse
flames with wet light, neck stretched ice-keen, mane
streaming, head bent in a perfect curve, a frozen wave
caught in mid-leap.

Big Crunching

"Why do we remember the past but not the future?... People in the contracting phase would live their lives backward..." Steven Hawking

Will the baby remember the twinge of arthritis?
Will the grape on the vine remember the pressure of the treader's foot,
    the warty slab of the taster's tongue?
Will the soldier remember the bite of the bullet with his name on it
    as he goes into the recruiting office
    with an unsuitable haircut and earring?
Will the seedling remember, as it splits the conker and writhes out,
    the scream of the chainsaw?
Will lovers remember their last kiss
    as their eyes meet for the first time?
Will the drunk remember the drying out clinic as he drops
    his cuddly pink elephant to sip from his father's glass?
Will the biscuit remember the steaming mug, its hot wet dunking,
    the dissolving of its crumbs
    while the wheat still grows, and the fat is being hydrogenated?
Will a woman remember the smell of her baby's neck
    while she forgets to buy condoms?
Will the kangaroo remember leather trainers
    bouncing along wet and gloomy pavements?

'Light is fast and lonely'

(Linda France)

1924: rocked in a cradle of stars, shielded
by the outflung arm of the Milky Way,
we slept, not knowing the bough
was broken.

Two million years before, the light set off,
a pulse from the heart of Andromeda,
streaking to earth while ape evolved
into astronomer.

From Mount Wilson
Hubble fielded it in his telescope,
let it burn into the plate, the image
of a nebula, stars in a cloudy net.
His frozen hands took home
the stars in negative, black
freckles on white sky.

When he saw and understood, the universe
we knew exploded into infinity,
galaxies still unfurling, hurtling apart.

We were falling all along,
a drop in an endless rainstorm,
through space that stretches,
curves and twists, even disappears,
and the Milky Way falls with us,
its light shed years ago.

Persephone

No sooner has the blood-warm seed
exploded in my mouth, my eyes
filled with dark, my limbs coiled
like pale strong roots and my heart
swollen like a winter bulb
than she
calls me back from my dark lover
into her world of trugs and trowels
and Gardener's Question Time.

Here he is laid out, waiting for me to bury him
with my hair, seal his mouth, cover his eyes,
wrap him like a warm shroud,
but she
calls me back, and I go, uprooted
by guilt, into the daytime world
of teas on the lawn and paisley-print
picnic rugs.

In the underworld I have power;
with her, I am once more the lost little girl
snatched by the vile seducer, taken
to the hell of what she calls
'the bedroom side of things.'
And she
will always call me back, and I will go,
until my longing for the rich juice
of pomegranates pulls me down
to him, and our earthy bed.

Atalanta

I was one fast woman, the best,
leaving the men for dead. Just me,
out in front, impaling myself on the wind,
blood pumping in my thighs, arms
hauling in the distance. He
ended up with the medal though.
Fouled the track, threw golden apples
at my feet. I nearly fell. Did fall
for him and his gold, while he shot past
winning me, and the race.

He was never better than second best,
we both knew it. But he went on winning,
and running, while I
merged with the blur of faces
cheering him on. Always there,
always thanked for my support
in his victory speeches.

But now I know he never gave up
chasing skirts, offering his golden balls
to stop women in their tracks. Rage
has inflated my lungs, hardened
my soft muscles, made me hungry
for racing,
for winning.

Circe

I would love it, if just once
I found a man
who did not become a pig,
bristly, snouting;
or a dog,
snarling and vicious
at my touch, pushing his wet nose
up my skirt.
This power I never asked for
condemns me to an insular life
and a diet of roast pork.
I had high hopes of Odysseus
but he was an animal in bed,
sweaty, flatulent, leaving crumbs
of crackling in the sheets. Worse,
I had to listen to him boasting,
then excusing, when it became clear
he in no way resembled a stallion,
as he had claimed.
It was a relief to see him go.
Still, I try them all out,
strapping sailors, pirates, heroes,
hoping my kiss
will humanise them.

Sirens

Yes, we do eat men.
There's nothing else to eat
on this barren island. Stranded,
all we want is to leave; we call,
our voices mourning fresh bread
warm as blood,
the plump cheeks of peaches.
We call, whenever a ship appears,
hoping at last for rescue. A boat,
some rope, fresh water, a chance
of escape. But each time,
the crews hear us
with sex-starved ears, see us
with woman-hungry eyes.
They never listen to our words,
they look at our bodies, then
desperate, stupid, dive overboard
and swim to us, bringing only their flesh.

Medusa

It was my beauty stopped men in their tracks,
though I never could believe in it myself.
They sought me out, a trophy for their manhood;
then my looks petrified them. They blamed me
of course. When I hid away, returned no calls,
they said I played with them. Not so. I hid in shame,
ugly as I felt myself to be. Mouth too big, hair
like a nest of snakes. I could not look in a mirror
without turning to stone. What woman can?
When Perseus came, I forgot my looks,
in gazing at his beauty. He had no trouble
believing it, hardly noticed me,
what with checking out his reflection
all the time. My turn to lose my head.

The woman whose husband mistook her for a hat

What is a wife for, if not to contain a man's thoughts?
They choose us to fit the size of their heads, wear us
as a symbol of their achievement. To many women
being mistaken for a hat should not seem odd:
I can cope with it, thought it is uncomfortable,
could even be lethal if he persists in his mistake.

More strange is how my house has become a zoo
of alien objects, his life a domestic safari. A glove
might be 'a change purse for coins of five sizes.'
His foot and shoe are indistinguishable; he pats
the head of the grandfather clock.

He has his music, though. He sings himself through
eating, dressing, holding his world together with a net
of harmony. He is still a lovely man. Sometimes I feel
his thoughts are really in my head. He was my lover, now
as I lay out his clothes, cut up his food,
I can easily mistake him for a child, whom I must forgive
for trying to wear me on his head.

On the Island of Achromatopsia

Our day is night but with a bigger moon
that bursts into the dark sky like a bomb.
Its brightness blurs the shapes inside my room,
the moving shadows' song is quite struck dumb.
Night comes, and brings our day, in which we hear
each word of moon and sea's soft conversation;
hunting the octopus beneath the ocean
I meet its gaze, through water deep but clear.
Fire is a dance, clouds melt into the sky.
Each object has its own particular radiance,
which catches light, returns it to my eye,
a symphony of meaning in each glance.
Colour's a myth. Our senses take delight
in listening to the language of pure light.

Rappel

There is always the possibility of deer
in the yellow sky that bells like a stag,
in wine that leaps, a gazelle in the mouth,
in words that branch and twist like antlers,
polished and spiky.
There's a whiff of hartshorn in the shying
of an unknown road; the stroke of velvet,
the soft eyes of roe deer in the scent
of warm chocolate,
the dotting of hooves in the sharp sting
of peppercorns.

Let us admit the possibility of joy;
let the heart leap like a hind,
let a new bar of soap be put
into our blind wet hand
like a fawn's muzzle,
let love flame
like a crown of antlers.

Rappel: 'reminder': from French roadsign warning of deer

28

Société Départementale de Papillons Blancs

(brass plate on French office building)

We have a department of wings
billowing
like blown muslin
creamy with pollen
like made-up eyelids
smudged with kohl

Then there is the department of flight
that flirts
with gravity, like clarinet notes
spiralling, or dust motes,
blundering
stumbling
like a beautiful woman
enchantingly drunk at a ball

Our department of tongues
curl like pubic hair, spring
straight to suck from sweet
places that are secret
drinking
with no need to swallow

The department of eyes
sees myriad views
all slightly different
through light rent
and shattered
like a frozen rainbow

We make summer a wing that beats
like a heart, creaming the eyelids
with pollen, choking the throat
with sweetness, splitting the light
like ice,
making the eyes
drunk with butterflies

Experiment on processional caterpillars

Round and round the caterpillars go
head to tail in circular formation;
they starve, while in their midst the green leaves grow.

I placed them round the pot's rim in a row –
a scientist, my role is observation;
round and round the caterpillars go.

I must not think how much they feel, or know,
I must be cold, just gathering information.
They starve, while in their midst the green leaves grow.

My wife's in bed, her skin a golden glow,
but I am rooted here. I must not leave my station
as round and round the caterpillars go.

Days pass; their endless march begins to slow,
they get no nearer to their destination,
they starve while in their midst the green leaves grow.

Not one steps out from that blind rippling flow
to eat the food that fuels their desperation;
still, round and round the caterpillars go.

My wife has gone; where, I don't know,
but the march of science is my justification –
see, they starve while in their midst the green leaves grow.

Day seven. All lie dead and shrivelled, so
no power of reason is the explanation.
That's why round and round the caterpillars go,
to starve while in their midst the green leaves grow.

On my computer

(from Shakespeare's sonnet 130)

My computer's screen is nothing like the sun
and yet it lights my way when all is dark.
It cannot walk, but I can make it run:
one touch, and it ignites as with a spark.
Whatever words I pour into its ear
it gives back to my eyes in equal measure.
The secrets of my heart I need not fear
to tell – they're guarded in its chest like treasure.
I love to hear its printer's artless chatter
which speaks my words in wholly senseless sound
it holds my mind, yet it is only matter:
though wired to earth, it's never touched the ground.
But when I ask return of my infatuation
it answers back: *Illegal Operation.*

Balloon Suicide

(from a small paragraph in *Bild*)

No-one in the basket saw him jump.
They were all looking up, perhaps.
One of them glimpsed his hat
follow him at a more leisurely pace,
then they realised his absence;
unnoticed while he was there, gone,
he was more conspicuous.
A few branches may have broken
as he vanished
into the indifferent forest; the police
who searched for him grumbled
about mosquitoes.

So if he chose the balloon trip
to be a last bold gesture, it failed
to make his mark. As he had.
No big drama: just no girlfriend,
no home of his own, and then no job.
Dying must have seemed
like the one thing he could do. Up there,
floating above his life, if he saw
the beauty of the sky, the trees,
it was not enough
to make up for it all – in the end
maybe he was more afraid to rise
than he was to fall.

Why me?

One day
you find a spider on your towel,
starred black into the fabric;
after that it's always there,
crouching,
to be found again.

Once you've met the man in the alley,
smelt his breath, known the spades of his hands,
his footsteps patrol
your dreams.

Once you've felt the impact of metal,
seen the road spin round you,
you feel the shock as every car you pass
hits you,
a flinching in the gut.

You've been skinned like meat,
stripped of that invisible membrane
which keeps you immune
until it's punctured, shredded, lost,
exposing your flesh to the truth:
there is no 'why me?'

There is only 'why not?'

Haiku

Beneath the graves, dead
coal mines cannot rest in peace;
headstones lie tumbled.

Rain on the pond tempts
the frog to surface for spring:
its eyes two bubbles.

The female blackbird
ferries hay into the hedge:
above, the male sings

The moon is too big,
too bright, too early, too round:
a shout in the sky.

From my back garden,
Venus, Jupiter, Saturn;
three steps to heaven.

Haring en Meisjes

The brochures are full of them; Dutch girls,
Gouda-gold hair, skin plump and creamy
as a young cow's udder,
their heads tipped back.
They love those fish,
raw, marinated herrings, gutted.
No chocolate flakes that soften
in the mouth for these Amazons,
no scented baths and ringing phones,
but the stiff, supple, silver bolt
sliding salty between their parted lips
as red and round as Edam cheeses
and down those strong white throats,
swallowed whole.

River blindness

Unlike our crops, we grow towards the dark.
The names of things we taste like fruit
held in the mouth, a scent
hinting at the shapes our memories hold.

The river is twisted rope
burning our hands as we feel our way,
hearing the sun flash
on endless skeins of water.

Growing older is learning to walk
daily more slowly,
using our ever-tasting hands,
groping into blackness.
We learn to let our children lead us,
lean on them, the smooth pebbles
of their shoulders warm under our fingers.

Our feet learn to stumble,
our toes smell their way
like the snouts of pigs
truffling through the dust.

Food is a warm breath on the face.
The brown drone of flies, the violet call of birds,
tickle our skin. We grow down,
seeking the darkness of roots coiling,
the comfort of the heartbeat,
holding our children's faces
sealed under our eyelids.

Winter Break

There's a swimming pool in blue mosaic –
they call it the 'leisure club',
but we don't need it. All afternoon
we swim in this four-poster,
slippery as fish.

Outside, the river shakes loose, stretches
as winter breaks its hold.
Cold water flows into the mouths of fish
that hang entranced to feel its fingers
stroke their sides.

Inside, we become each other's river,
strong enough to carry away whole trees,
gentle enough to feel the smallest minnow
winnow its fins deep down.
White crusty towels like snowy banks
wait for our otter-sleek bodies
to land themselves, breathe air
alive with river-light.

Moonbathing

My lover has been moonbathing.
On warm, soft summer nights
he smoothed a total moonblock
all over his naked body,
forgetting his buttocks. Then
he lay under the moon,
beguiled, languid as a lizard
in that wash of cool white heat
for far too long. Now moonburn
makes that perfect bottom glow
between his golden back and thighs,
like a tight new mushroom enticed
from the earth by moonlight. I
warm it with my hot brown hands.

Writing a Mills and Boon

One day, short of cash, I decided to write a romance.
The next day, I'd write another.
But it wasn't that easy. Even though my hero was tall,
dark, arrogant, and bulging with male hardness.
(But there was more to him than that – inside,
he seethed with hard maleness.) My heroine
was flame-haired, petite but feisty. She would try to hate him,
but be disturbed by his magnificent torso. They would fight,
kiss deeply (Chapter Three), fall out again, have sex
(with simultaneous orgasms) in Chapter Eight: part
through a misunderstanding, then (Chapter Ten) declare
undying love.

But they began to give me trouble. She
kept wanting to go clubbing with the girls; when he seized her
she didn't melt against him, but blacked his eye, filed
a complaint of sexual harassment. He
was always hanging about where she wasn't, flashing
his teeth and muscles, until he told me, masterfully,
of his innate need to be dominated. A need only I
with my all-powerful fingers could fulfil. I told him
there was someone else, but he followed me
onto every page. Fed up, I wrote them both onto a beach,
switched off and left them to sort it out.

But the other night I saw her in a minidress with a gang of girls,
going noisily into a seafront wine bar – she even waved –
and someone keeps leaving silent messages
on my answerphone.

Einstein's daughter

I know the laws of relativity: everything depends
on the observer's viewpoint. A child is a joy,
or a shame, when marriage is the frame of reference.
But why did my father doubt that God plays dice,
when he created me by random chance?
He rejected me along with the uncertainty principle.
I took it with me – I know the universe is built on it,
I, whose whole identity is uncertain. I wonder
if he ever thought of me, or do geniuses prefer
to forget their mistakes? I have the picture of him
sticking out his tongue at the press, as he did at Hitler.
If only he had learned to do it sooner, he might
have clung to me. Instead, he clung
to the universal constant, another mistake, but one
he would not give up. I know
there is no such thing. Even a mother, a father
is not always constant. Would he be proud,
to know I have inherited his brain?
He ceased to value my mother's, abandoned her
and my brothers too, yet spoke like a poet
and a saint. Which of my fathers is real?
It all depends on your point of view,
on the principle of relativity.

Toothache, heartache

My dentist has left me.
She called me by my name each time,
        without consulting notes.
She said my teeth were beautiful,
and gave me all the credit for it.
I felt beautiful and clever
        each time I left her.

When nothing needed doing, I shared her joy;
when something did, she ached with the pain
        her skill denied me.

Then she was gone, without a word.
Efficient young men manhandle my teeth
        lovelessly now.

But I remember her
encircling my head with dedicated fingers
her legs around my chair
as if about to play a cello.

Bones from a medic's dustbin

I hold this human spine like a rosary of bone,
fingering the winged vertebrae.
I stack them to nest snugly
in totem poles of little trolls;
spread them to examine
the delicate neck rings,
the beaky thoracic vertebrae
which held the ribs, the massive
cushions of the lumbar bones
which carried, strained and ached,
and the shield-shaped pubic bone
like the head of a knobby snake.

I fit it to my body all the way up;
at least my size, and closer to me now
than ever lovers were. But all my touching
of this body's stem can't tell me
whether man or woman, young or old,
but I can guess, poor, and probably Third World,
dark as their bones are milky
like white Aero. Western skeletons
cannot be bought and sold.

I think of this spine cocked to one side
to hoist a child, bent under hot, hard work,
twisted by pain, stretched out in sleep
and hope that once some fingers counted
the bumps in the living back, gently as mine do now.

Don't put your daughter into space, Mrs Kirk

What happens to old spacewomen? Or even, slightly middle aged?
In the future of equal opportunities, no job is closed to women
(save Captain).
They rocket up, chief this, commander that,
while barely in their twenties; heads,
we presume, full of micro-circuits, they sway
the shining corridors of starships, in skin-tight catsuits.

But while the men, of varying handsomeness, spread, go grey,
and dare to baldly go where no woman has before
(towards an old age pension)
they disappear. Sent home perhaps to breed
their brains and beauty into future crews,
or jettisoned in hyper-space, like garbage.
Perhaps beamed down to some obscure planet, to join
a crowd of aging women with degrees in astro-physics
discovering the joy of leaving their mascara off.

It must be hard to save the ship from aliens, all the while
waiting for the signal to drop out of active service,
being no longer quite so ornamental.
Does a specially assigned ship's officer scan
the female personnel, alert for wrinkles or a sagging bum?
Do they go quietly, unasked, but warned by instinct
like elephants did (when there were elephants):
or screaming, bundled out the airlock
while the camera's elsewhere?

It will remain a mystery, like Dr Who's toilet.
But better to kill them, Captain. Or else one day,
an angry maenad-horde of beautiful old women
will storm your bridge, knowing exactly where
to pull your plug out.

Ann More: Mrs John Donne

I thought myself a lucky woman then –
to capture such a poet, such a lover,
so skilful with his hands, his tongue, his pen…
I, his America, he, eager to discover.
A secret marriage; his imprisonment,
his risked career, and all for love of me!
I little knew my long confinement
would end too soon – released at thirty-three.
But babies came, twelve times I waxed and waned.
While he would beg the unruly sun stand still,
I prayed in secret to the moon, complained
of headache, backache, feeling tired and ill.
In one black year, a son and daughter died;
the child inside me kicked me as I cried.

Oh, I did love him, but the easy pleasure
two lovers in one bed, one mind, enjoy
popped like that saucy flea; instead, I'd measure
the long, slow, swollen months to girl or boy.
And he did love me, always, bride and mother,
despite the distorted shape his love had filled.
Only his God could take my place, no other,
when I and my last child his love had killed.
I know mine is a woman's common story;
but would have liked to share the acclaim he won,
lived longer, seen my children's growth, his glory –
a lucky woman, though my life was Donne.
But he gave to poems, I to babies, breath:
his labour brought him fame, mine brought me death.

The fate of the spineless

On the screen the image glows moon-bright
tucked up safe and warm in restful night,
each starfish hand, whorled ear, and skin-sealed eye
reflected by the spine in perfect symmetry.

But the spine itself is flawed; the daylit skies
will never show their colours to those eyes.
To perfect babies we must all aspire,
consigning those unfinished to the fire.

The growth of life and mind's beyond our art:
how cells divide to form the head and heart,
why having formed, the heart begins to beat,
why limb-buds branch and flower, hands and feet.

Some links are missing in the silver chain
which forms a curving ladder to the brain
of this one child whose reach exceeds his grasp,
like a string of pearls with badly mended clasp.

On the screen the image glows moon-bright
to be extinguished, lost in endless night.
No light will ever quicken that sealed eye;
that bifid spine, imperfect symmetry.

The heart does not break when bones do

My heart used to beat in the swift,
sharp tap of my high heels,
pecking out the rhythm of my blood. Now
heart and feet are out of step,
out of tune: my halting, muffled feet
pluck painful notes, to the percussion
of two sticks; a patter of uncertain rain.

But the heart does not break
when bones do. It holds firm
at the core, sound as an apple,
candid as a barn owl's
heart-shaped, apple-slice face.

My heart still hammers out the powerful beat
That used to find expression in my feet.

Bateson's Belfry

Not death I fear, but life beyond the grave,
that last black loneliness,
eyes open to the dark, my screams
silenced by a massive plug of earth.

In my workshop, warm scent
of wood curls, linseed oil
flowing like honey

By comforting the poor, I grew rich;
even they will buy a belfry,
tie the rope's end to the cold still hand.
Above the box, a bell whose tongue
can give the dead a voice,
bring them back to light.

Rich the golden oil,
brightening the pale surface

But I cannot be comforted. No contrivance
is infallible. While I still hold the reins,
I choose the one sure way to escape
the dark, the cold, the damp. Myself my coffin,
in a blaze of oil-fed light, safe at last.

Golden my oiled skin, golden the flame,
its hot breath welcome on my cheek.
The bells will toll my triumph over the earth

A celebration of lost punchlines

Forget the punchline! I like best
the first lines of jokes, the ones
that set the scene, place us
in a world where anything can happen.

A horse goes into a pub;
does it matter
if the barman forgets to say,
'Why the long face?'
Not to me. I'm happy to see it there,
leaning its patient muzzle on the bar,
next to a rhino
who's complaining about the price of beer.

I'd rather live in a world
where two peanuts walk down Picadilly
and neither of them is assaulted;
where men go about in trios
of assorted nationalities
for no particular reason. Why should I care
what the big chimney said to the little chimney,
as long as they keep talking
up there against the cold sky?

I'm just wondering
how I'll know
if there's an elephant in bed with me.

Showing Herr Hitler my new shoes

(home movie, Berchtesgarten)

Herr Hitler is a nice kind man,
he'll save us from the nasty Jews,
because my Mummy says he can.
I will show him my new shoes.

They are fat and black and shiny,
even underneath is clean.
They are new and they are mine, he
sees what a good girl I've been.

His cheeks are pink like my doll's bottom,
his smile is white, his moustache black.
He wears a cap and shiny buttons.
He smiles at me, so I smile back.

He bows, his warm hand holds my hand,
he nods and smiles to see my feet.
I lift my legs high one by one,
I hope he'll give me something sweet.

Herr Hitler loves all girls and boys.
He'll save us from those nasty Jews,
monsters who will steal my toys.
I'm glad I showed him my new shoes.

There's no such thing as society

(an updating of John Betjeman)

Phone for my prozac, Saffron,
for my aura's a little unnerved.
The house rabbit's peed on the supplements,
and the Chardonnay's too warm to be served.
Are the aubergines all in the aga?
The sun-dried tomatoes can wait
till the au pair's replenished the water feature,
and sawn some more logs for the grate.
Pine decking's just right, and not too dear,
so the patio's perfect for tea;
Tarquin's out buffing his bullbars,
so do come and have some with me.
I've got some authentic Thai pastries,
the monks knead the dough with bare feet!
I hope you don't mind if I ask you –
face the door, good feng shui, my sweet.
Now, no milk, and the lemon's unwaxed, dear
yes, those are my new crystal stones.
Oh god! my woman's bought doileys –
let's call them ironic. Now, scones?

Eating Cadbury's Mini-rolls

We had Cadbury's mini-rolls with tea:
the chocolate coating crazed, flaked off
as it always does. We chased the pieces
with licked fingertips, our places at the table
marked by sweet brown crumbs.

But our guests, two women who were blind,
stopped speaking, using all their skill to eat
so not one crumb was dropped.

It mattered to them, not to make a mess,
appear inept and childish. They could not see
how their superb efficiency set them apart –
nor see us watch the beauty of their hands
in perfect mastery of chocolate and gold foil.

Trench Experience

(Imperial War Museum)

In darkness we walked through
the rats, the blam and thud of shells,
the mud walls made of resin.
Young men in effigy spoke endlessly
on tape loops
reading letters home, calling for help,
ignoring us, as if we were the ghosts.

And so we were. No mud stuck to our shoes.
Our clothes were dry, no seeping corpses
reeked – just a faint miasma, like Elsan.
There was no fear.
Moved, impressed, gasping for tea,
we headed for clean toilets and
shockingly priced cakes.

They couldn't have done it better,
without putting the tourists off. Fair's fair.

But Great-great Uncle, when we visited next day,
flooded it for us with his memories.
The guilt of being still alive and whole
when all your friends are dead or
shot apart. Knowing you are next.
His third time into battle, both feet shattered,
his bleeding into mud for hours and hours:
being kept alive on drops of best champagne,
less precious then than water.

53

"Your Great-Grandma would have been good at Maths

Slice after slice, she has dished up her sleep to them,
keeping only the smallest piece for herself.
Now, tiredness keeps her warm, like fur.
        She's up before dawn, alone,
to make a shirt before breakfast
or there will be no dinner. A simple daily sum:
Small dead sighs from the just-cold range;
white linen gathers the light, and makes it gleam.
        She warms her eyes at it.
Her thickened fingers barely feel the needle
as it slips like a fish through the cloth –
tiny stitches unroll in hundreds, like eggs
        piped from a queen bee's sting.

Obedient as ironing, the shirt takes shape.
Into it, she sews her thirteen children,
her man's shipyard thirst for beer
his rages and spent wage packets
and strangely, her luxury, numbers,
dancing through the needleholes in daisychains;
playing their tricks like toddlers in her head
        as she knocks back bread,
        hefts steaming sheets from the copper,
        leads the range with silver black.
Upstairs, bairns call, his braces drag
on floorboards. The shirt is finished,
fit for man to wear and woman to wash.
Her child, my grandma, takes it,
runs down the road for the money;
her survival, then her twins', then
my luxurious education, and
my children's choice-filled lives:

        While she begins her working day.

54

You're never too poor to buy soap

My Grandma was hard. Gritty as Vim, or the rice
she chewed, raw, to keep her hunger down.
Her twins were fed, kept clean, expected to clear their plates
and kiss her stony cheek at bedtime, like a punishment.
Inside her, churning like lava, love
for her husband and children, contempt for his unemployment,
ambition for her son, but mostly pride.

So she scrubbed and scoured the shameful marks of poverty away
and no-one knew if she cried with weariness and fear
sometimes over the washing.

She weakened, once. A guilty lapse, like a dirty weekend.
Desperate, she went to the clinic where middle-class women
qualified for social work by leisure and smart hats
doled out free baby food to the deserving poor.

Smart as a one-woman army surrendering with honour
she brandished her children, miracles of patching and contriving,
determined to appear as good as anyone.
It was a mistake.
The woman liked her poor shabby, in the dust, preferably whining,
said no, called her a scrounger, said she couldn't be in need
if she could look so neat and clean.

Like acid in the face. The burn of guilt and shame
hardened her to marble as she pushed the polished pram back home.

She lived to ninety-one, saw her children rich by Byker standards,
softened into talcum (Ashes of Roses),
but her brillo pad mothering left scratches
no duster could wipe off.

Summer 1940, End of term

She's walking home from school as slowly as she dares
without dawdling. The silence she dreads most,
her mother's expert disapproval of her news.
The dinner plate put down to her
will echo like a slap
in that house where three day's silence mourns
a cracked cup. But it's all in the school report:
top of the class again. A pretty girl, disfigured
by the brain which should have been her brother's,
she has usurped his chance
to lift them all from poverty, pay back
his mother's heavy loan of love.

Nearly home. She wonders why she tries so hard
to please them all, in everything but this –
why she can't misbehave, except to do her best
at school. It is her one rebellion.

Second Sex

Child of a twin, I half-expected twins.
When I knew the bairn was single,
still I thought of it as two;
a boy, and/or a girl, both named

I had a son already; would not admit a bias either way
    for this one
      hugging it inside,
protecting it from expectations
of what was fitting for a second child.

My daughter's sex was born before her head.
"It's a girl!" they said, as I cried
"Is it alive?" Those little legs stuck up
from my opened belly a moment,
like someone doing hand-stands in a swimming pool,
and then I saw her wide-eyed startled face.

My lovely girl! and with her birth
a tiny, quiet death:
that of the boy she might have been,
slipping away almost unnoticed
from the birthday celebrations.

I had just what I wanted
but when people said so
    openly
(you must be pleased to have a girl
this time, it's best
to have one of each)
I felt a rush of indignation
for my ghost-son;
had to stop myself defending him aloud.

First Choice

Leeds, or UEA? My son sits
Hunched in his adolescent chrysalis
Over the UCAS form. We've read
The prospectuses, (prospecti?),
Compared excellence ratings,
Employment records, crime figures.
They've made him the same offers,
More or less. So it's between the two.

Entranced, I pore over nightclubs,
Student-friendly restaurant adverts,
Seeing myself there. I remember
My first time, the dreaming spires
Of Geordieland, lying under a tree
In daisy-drenched grass drinking wine,
Gazing at someone's profile
While a slim ribbon of smoke snaked
Up into the willows... or did I
Read all that in Evelyn Waugh,
Dunking cheap teabags and gingersnaps
While the football crowds bellowed
Harsh poetry from the terraces?

Now, UEA or Leeds? And suddenly
I realise, all over the country,
Girls sit, girls like his schoolfriends,
Organised, focused, powerful,
Deciding, UEA or Manchester? LSE
Or Leeds? One of them
Is choosing my son
As she ticks, he ticks, Leeds;
A girl who'll break his heart,
Or make him happy: a girl
I'll have to love.

Fruitless

When I bit the sinewy backbones from satsuma segments –
dissected and flayed oranges, pecking out the pips,
and fed them to my daughter one by one:
when I sliced the buttocks off crisp green apples,
leaving the core and bitter seeds, and
gave them salivating to my son,
I wished they could manage their fruit themselves.

And now they can.

And now I want to peel and prise apart
their lives, rip out
all that's bitter, all that chokes,
see what seeds are inside
waiting to grow.

But I can't.

English Heritage

1. EXHIBITS, HAWORTH PARSONAGE

Charlotte's wedding bonnet is empty now,
but a shy riot of grey lace flowers
still celebrates the end of long waiting,
the beginning of a life. A few
lilies-of-the-valley have almost escaped.

Her baby's bonnet is turned to the wall;
finely worked lace, white as lilies,
it is tiny, perfect, and empty.

2. PUTTING A STOP TO THE PRIDE AND PREJUDICE INDUSTRY

It is a truth universally acknowledged
that the single man in possession of a good fortune
who has just taken Netherfield
is having an affair
with that tall, proud chap from Derbyshire.

We have to talk

He spoke forcefully,
persuasively, assertively,
allegorically, vividly,
coherently, and with a
masterly use of body language.
Finally, he sat back, hands
spread conclusively, and said
removing a flake of earwax
with a fingernail, "Well,
that's it. I've made my
position absolutely clear."

Vaguely, absently, she asked,
"So what is your position?"

White Skin

Smooth as a racehorse's rump
he groomed the primed and undercoated wood
before he began the gloss.
Hand tense with control, he oiled over
every rib of grain with brilliant white
as he talked of his sons with pride.
Not a drop hit the carpet,
not a dribble marred the work
as he stretched the paint from edge
to exact edge, the brush relentless
as his voice, abrasive now, stripped bare
a philosophy of rope, lash, death at birth
for undesirables. He bound the door
like a book, with a taut, sleek hide
of whitest skin.

On his mobile phone

Still I must tell my secrets to her
even though she is killing me
as she listens, whispers back
the assurances I need – tells me
I am here, in this train, I am me,
in the crowd, I am not alone, in my car.
I am nothing
without the heft of her, her weight
warming in my hand. Her face
lights up for me. No-one else
does that. So when she calls,
I answer. When I need to talk,
I reach for her, knowing
she will enter me,
flickering through my brain
like sheet-lightning, chasing
my thoughts down endless corridors
with a light that burns.

She etches her name in dead nerve-cells
with a delicate laser. I cannot read it
but I feel it there, her mark on me
like Calais carved on the queen's heart.

Each time I hold her to my ear
she penetrates more deeply,
hunting down my memories,
erasing as she goes.

When she is silent, a smooth stone
in my pocket, the light goes out;
but the damage she has done
still glows in me, painless,
welcome. "You're killing me,"
I whisper, "do it, yes."

63

Package

Herded at Heathrow, penned in by noise
and newstands, she waited to be called
for the holiday of a lifetime.
"Look after this for me?" – a woman swooped,
dumped a bag of cameras on her lap, and
freed, took off towards the exit kiosk.

Like being given a present, not for opening;
the warmth she felt came purely from the giving,
being singled out for trust. She sat on,
cradling the package, waiting
while time ticked on, slow seconds running out.